THE
JOURNEY TO GREATNESS

MOGOMOTSI JACKY KABELO

The Journey to Greatness

"…..But the people that do know their God shall be strong, and do great exploits".

Daniel 11:32

Mogomotsi Jacky Kabelo

Author's contact details:

Mogomotsi Jacky Kabelo
P. O. Box 46115, Gaborone, Botswana
Plot 39116, Block 6, Gaborone, Botswana
Email: mogomotsikabelo@yahoo.com
Tel: +267 3922240
Cell: +267 74959306 / +267 71532284

Publisher
Self

Editorial & Editing
Dr Kabelo D. Mokgacha
Mrs Onneile P. Lempadi
Ms Esther M. Mpete

ISBN NO: 978-99968-0-233-1

Unless otherwise stated, all Scripture quotations are taken from the King James Version of the Bible. The scriptures marked
AMP are from Amplified bible and the ones marked HCSB are from Holman Christian Standard Bible.

Disclaimer

Copyright © 2014 Mogomotsi Jacky Kabelo

Graphic Designer

Universal Prints
Reginald Mabote
uniqprints@gmail.com
Cell: +267 71580304

Printed & Bound by

Printing & Publishing Company Botswana (PTY) LTD
Plot 5647, Nakedi Rd, Broadhurst Industrial
P. O. Box 130, Gaborone
sales@ppcb.co.bw

DEDICATION

I dedicate this book to my lovely wife, Precious Jessica, and our three sons– Faith Tinashe, Kagiso Joseph and Prince Phatsimo– who have always shown me love and support throughout the authoring of this book. Thank you very much for allowing me to answer the call of God upon my life at the expense of all the time I should have spent with you. I am eternally grateful to God for having brought you into my life.

ACKNOWLEDGEMENTS

I remain indebted to all those who heard me express these principles when I first shared them in my sermons and urged me to turn them into a book. A huge thank you to the Faith Covenant Ministry family for their unshakable support, blessings and for being a great audience; may God do good in your lifetime.

Most of all let me appreciate my wife, friend and partner in ministry who has always provided a shoulder for me to cry on during difficult times in ministry and throughout the writing of this book. I love you girl.

I want to thank my parents (Mr Keratwe & Mrs Basadi G. Kabelo) for all that they have invested in my life with the little resources they had, may God bless you for your patience.

I thank Mr Reginald Mabote, of Universal Prints, for

designing the covers of this book. I also want to acknowledge my spiritual father, Apostle Percival J. Mtetwa, for the impact that he has had in my life over the years in my spiritual journey. You have been such a great father.

I also want to thank Bishop Dr. Dag Heward Mills who through his books and tapes has radically changed my life. Apostle Margret "Mama" Mhlanga thank you for your support in the work of the ministry. Thank you very much for exposing me to a broader scope of ministry.

To many other servants of God who have influenced my life in this spiritual journey thanks to you all. And finally a huge thank you to my heavenly Father for the gift of life and the gift of salvation. I am eternally grateful for all that you have made me to be and for being the God that is not a respecter of persons. Glory to God in the highest.

Table of Contents

INTRODUCTION

A life of greatness is an exceptional life which an individual attains by finding the perfect-will of God for their life, and doing everything it takes through God's power to fulfil their God-given mandate in this life. Every individual is born with the ability within them to become great in their own right; this ability is normally referred to as 'potential'.

In the scriptures, God speaks clearly to his servant Jeremiah about potential;

"Before I formed thee in the belly I knew thee; and before thou camest forth out of the womb I sanctified thee, and I ordained thee a prophet unto the nations."

Jeremiah 1:5

What this simply means is that even before the Prophet Jeremiah knew about what he was capable of doing, the ability to do it was already infused into his system. In other words, Jeremiah had the potential to become what he was not yet aware he was able to become. Potential means untapped ability or capable of development into actuality which is within an individual. Jeremiah only needed a push from God in order for him to realize that he was a gifted individual and to even start walking in the direction of that greatness.

In this book we follow the story of Abraham as he was challenged by God to make a sacrifice for Him of his son Isaac, the only child he had from his God-ordained matrimonial home. We will explore, revelationally, different steps along that journey which helped Abraham reach the ultimate place which God had intended for his life. It is an obvious fact that God will always shift us from our comfort zone in order for him to bring us to the extraordinary. I trust that God will supernaturally transform your life as you go through this book. Try the steps in this book and see your life change from glory to glory. Amen.

PREFACE

The journey to greatness was birthed from the study of the life of Abraham and his unshakable faith in the Lord, even when God asked him to do the most difficult thing imaginable to any human being; to take his only son and offer him as a sacrifice to God. Simply put, God asked Abraham to kill his only matrimonial child, and I just wonder how many of us could have managed to obey God to this degree. But Abraham obeyed and there are several things that we can learn from him; his attitude, tenacity, interpersonal skills and how he went about the whole process, just to mention but a few things that made him to emerge as one of the greatest men that ever lived on this planet. In my view this is one of the greatest stories in the bible for one to learn from.

1 And it came to pass after these things that God did tempt Abraham, and said unto him, Abraham: and he said, Behold, *here* I *am.* 2

And he said, Take now thy son, thine only *son* Isaac, whom thou lovest, and get thee into the land of Moriah; and offer him there for a burnt offering upon one of the mountains which I will tell thee of. 3 And Abraham rose up early in the morning, and saddled his ass, and took two of his young men with him, and Isaac his son, and clave the wood for the burnt offering, and rose up, and went unto the place of which God had told him. 4 Then on the third day Abraham lifted up his eyes, and saw the place afar off. 5 And Abraham said unto his young men, Abide ye here with the ass; and I and the lad will go yonder and worship, and come again to you. 6 And Abraham took the wood of the burnt offering, and laid *it* upon Isaac his son; and he took the fire in his hand, and a knife; and they went both of them together. 7 And Isaac spake unto Abraham his father, and said, My father: and he said, Here *am* I, my son. And he said, behold the fire and the wood: but where *is* the lamb for a burnt offering? 8 And Abraham said, My son, God will provide himself a lamb for a burnt offering: so they went both of them together. 9 And they came to the place which God had told him of; and Abraham built an altar there, and laid the wood in order, and bound Isaac his son, and laid him on the altar upon the wood. 10 And Abraham stretched forth his hand, and took the knife to slay his son. 11 And the angel of the LORD called unto him out of heaven, and said, Abraham, Abraham: and he said, Here *am* I. 12 And he said, Lay not thine hand upon the lad, neither do thou anything unto him: for now I know that thou fearest God, seeing thou hast not withheld thy son, thine only *son* from me. 13 And Abraham lifted up his eyes, and looked, and behold behind *him* a ram caught in a thicket by his horns: and Abraham went and took the ram, and offered him up for a burnt offering in the stead of his son. 14 And Abraham called the name of that place Jehovahjireh: as it is said *to* this day, In the mount of the LORD it shall be seen. 15 And the angel of the LORD called unto Abraham out of heaven the second time, 16 And said, By myself have I sworn, saith the LORD, for because thou hast done this thing, and hast not withheld thy son, thine only *son:* 17 That in blessing I will bless thee, and in multiplying I will multiply thy seed as the stars of the heaven, and as the sand which *is* upon the sea shore; and thy seed shall possess the gate of his enemies; 18 And in thy seed shall all the nations of the earth be blessed; because thou hast obeyed my voice. 19 So Abraham returned unto his young men, and they rose up and went together to Beersheba; and Abraham dwelt at Beersheba.

Genesis 22:1-19

Chapter 1

THE POWER OF PLANNING

According to the story in Genesis it is very clear that when Abraham started off in his journey he took all the necessary things that he needed for the assignment that he was going to perform. He also knew his expected destination. He didn't just take off and hope that he will see when he gets there. It is rather very clear that Abraham planned for what he was going to do and how he was going to do it. He actually knew how many days it will take him to arrive at the expected destination.

3 And Abraham rose up early in the morning, and saddled his ass, and took two of his

young men with him, and Isaac his son, and clave the wood for the burnt offering, and rose up, and went unto the place of which God had told him. 4 Then on the third day Abraham lifted up his eyes, and saw the place afar off. 5 And Abraham said unto his young men, Abide ye here with the ass; and I and the lad will go yonder and worship, and come again to you. 6 And Abraham took the wood of the burnt offering, and laid *it* upon Isaac his son; and he took the fire in his hand, and a knife; and they went both of them together.

Genesis 22:36

Success is not an accident; it does not just happen to you. Don't ever expect to have any level of achievement without planning for it. No one will ever plan your life for you. A dream you don't work towards never becomes a reality. You can't become a goal-getter unless you are a goal-setter. All people who have a certain amount of success in life always do their home work.

Planning and mapping your way to your destination is an essential part of the journey to greatness. The word of God has this to say about people who don't know how to get where they are going in life.

15 The labour of the foolish wearieth every one of them, because he knoweth not how to go to the city. 16 Woe to thee, O land, when thy king is a child, and thy princes eat in the morning!

Ecclesiastes 10:15-16

It is very true that when you don't know how to get where you are going you weary the people around you who are even trying to help you. That's why in business there is even the concept of a business plan. Before the financial institution can lend you money, they want to know what you want to spend the money on and how you are going to make profit and eventually pay them back. If your plan is not good enough your application will not be successful because the bank knows that a poor plan produces poor results. So before we can talk about many other things we have to establish that this part of your life is in order. Do you have a plan in place for journey you are embarking upon?

28 For which of you, intending to build a tower, sitteth not down first, and counteth the cost, whether he have to finish it? 29 Lest haply, after he hath laid the foundation, and

is not able to finish it, all that behold it begin to mock him, 30 Saying, this man began to build, and was not able to finish.

Luke 14:2830

The journey to greatness is for people who start and finish what they started; if you only start and don't finish well your labour will be in vain.

8 Better is the end of a thing than the beginning thereof: and the patient in spirit is better than the proud in spirit.

Ecclesiastes 7:8

Build a habit of starting and finishing anything that you start. Many of us hardly gets anything done because we think we still have a lot of time at our disposal.

Did you know?
The average life span of a person is around 70 years. There are 25 550 days in that period of time. If a person sleeps 9 hours a day by the end of that week, which is 7 days, they would have slept 3 days of their lives away. This amounts to about 25 years of sleep in 70 years of life, leaving that individual with only 45 years of life. This does not take into

account the fact that when you where a baby you slept much longer than that and hence most of that time were not put to good use. The other thing that we have to put in perspective is that at 40 years you will have used 14 600 days of your life, remaining with about 10 950 days if you are to live for 70 years. *Food for thought.*

Many people think that they have a lot of time and hence they waste their lives moving in circles. The above breakdown can actually help us to realise that we don't have any time to waste.

Since we have established beyond any reasonable doubt that planning is crucial in order to arrive at the desired destination, let us go into some practical things that can help you to plan. There are different stages of life which I want to explore so that we can be able to know where we stand in the spectrum of life, this should be able to help us in our planning. These stages are the expected moves through life that each and every individual has to follow. For purposes of understanding, we are going to continue using seventy years as the average life span of an average person. If you are trusting God for immortality please don't be offended just read on you may learn something that will change your life forever.

We are going to look at the following stages; the learning stage (*morning*), the earning stage (*afternoon*), the turning stage (*evening*) and, finally, life after death (*night*).

1. THE LEARNING STAGE (MORNING)

This season of one's life is expected to fall between the first days of your life to about twenty five years of age. The bible is very clear that there is the morning stage of one's life.

16 Woe to thee, O land, when thy king is a child, and thy princes eat in the morning!

Ecclesiastes 10:16

According to scripture this is not the time for one to be busy eating and wasting resources, it is rather the time to be investing and developing oneself. During this time you are expected to learn all the basics of life and get enough qualifications and credentials for the next stage of your life.

At this stage you should:

- Get connected to God
- Be matured and understand the basics of life
- Complete your formal education and become a graduate
- Discover your vision and purpose in life
- Discover your career or area of focus and all you need to pursue that career
- You must be fully set for the next stage.

If you are twenty five years old and you don't have a vision and purpose for your life you are heading for disaster. For example, if you are still waiting to get admission into college or university or you are yet to get a career or a certificate to work with, then your life is already operating behind schedule, you need to speed up things.

Things to empower yourself with at this stage;

— Academic education
— Professional education
— Financial education
— Personal education (interpersonal skills)
— Spiritual education

Just as an example, I got the following from my

son's school report and it emphasises how going to school can develop your interpersonal skills.

The child,
- Is courteous
- Gets along well with others
- Exhibits self control
- Does not disturb others
- Shows respect for authority
- Responds well to correction

Schools monitor and nurture these social habits at an early age. It is amazing when you look into the world of business and life in general how applicable these simple social habits are, and how they determine our rising and falling in life. So when others go to school go also. The following verses of scripture show us how important it is to invest in one's life at the right time.

6 Go to the ant, thou sluggard; consider her ways, and be wise: 7 Which having no guide, overseer, or ruler, 8 Provideth her meat in the summer, and gathereth her food in the harvest.9 How long wilt thou sleep, O sluggard? When wilt thou arise out of thy sleep? 10 Yet a little sleep, a little slumber, a little folding of the

hands to sleep: 11 so shall thy poverty come as one that travelleth, and thy want as an armed man.

Proverbs 6:6-11

The ants understand times and seasons, and we also must be able to understand times and seasons of life if we are to emerge great in this life.

2. THE EARNING STAGE (AFTERNOON)

This second stage of life falls between the ages of twenty five and fifty years. The word of God spells this very clearly in the following verse of scripture.

23 And the Lord spake unto Moses, saying, 24 This is it that belongeth unto the Levites: from *twenty and five years old* and upward they shall go into wait upon the service of the tabernacle of the congregation: 25 And from the age of *fifty years* they shall cease waiting upon the service thereof, and shall serve no more: 26 But shall minister with their brethren in the tabernacle of the congregation, to keep the charge, and shall do no service. Thus shalt thou do unto the Levites touching their charge.

Numbers 8:23-26

During this stage of life you are expected to be earning a living and earning income from the investment you made in the previous season. The above scripture makes it very clear that even the people who worked for God; He needed them to fall within this category because He knows that during this time of one's life he or she has the strength and ability to serve him. So at this stage you should be using what you learnt from the first stage to earn a living and produce fruit in your life.

At this stage you should be;
- Living and burning for God, passionately
- Be married
- A parent and raising your children at this stage
- Using financial intelligence to secure your future
- At your maximum and prime productivity
- Buying property and investing at this stage of your life.

If at this stage you are still trying to pursue formal education, trying to get a degree, seeking a career to settle for, taking life for granted, void of investment mentality, you are operating below standard and you are behind schedule.

If you marry at fifty years when will you have and raise children. Do you still want to be changing diapers at sixty and taking children to school?

3. THE TURNING STAGE (EVENING)

This is the last stage of life; it falls between fifty and seventy or more years if you live longer.

At this stage it is expected that you should have gained financial independence and relaxed (some call it retirement). This is the stage when you turn around and begin to mentor and impact the next generation with your wealth of knowledge and experience.

You should not:
- Be nursing a baby at this stage except as a grandparent
- Be looking for a job
- Be in school except if you are doing it for fun
- Definitely be unmarried at this stage, except if you choose to or lost your spouse
- Be poor at this stage
- Be a tenant at this stage (still renting a house)

- Be an enemy of God at this stage or else you die

and end up in hell and all your life will have become a useless existence

4. LIFE AFTER DEATH (NIGHT)

One day Jesus made a very disturbing statement:

4 I must work the works of him that sent me, while it is day: the night cometh, when no man can work.

John 9:4

The Lord Jesus did not deny the fact that at some point in life there comes a night, in which no man can work. Where you spend eternity is determined by the choices you make while you are still alive.

19 There was a certain rich man, which was clothed in purple and fine linen, and fared sumptuously every day: 20 And there was a certain beggar named Lazarus, which was laid at his gate, full of sores, 21 And desiring to be fed with the crumbs which fell from the rich man's table: moreover the dogs

came and licked his sores. 22 And it came to pass, that the beggar died, and was carried by the angels into Abraham's bosom: the rich man also died, and was buried; 23 And in hell he lift up his eyes, being in torments, and seeth Abraham afar off, and Lazarus in his bosom. 24 And he cried and said, Father Abraham, have mercy on me, and send Lazarus that he may dip the tip of his finger in water, and cool my tongue; for I am tormented in this flame. 25 But Abraham said, Son, remember that thou in thy lifetime receivedst thy good things, and likewise Lazarus evil things: but now he is comforted, and thou art tormented. 26 And beside all this, between us and you there is a great gulf fixed: so that they which would pass from hence to you cannot; neither can they pass to us that would come from thence. 27Then he said, I pray thee therefore, father, that thou wouldest send him to my father's house: 28 For I have five brethren; that he may testify unto them, lest they also come into this place of torment. 29 Abraham saith unto him, they have Moses and the prophets; let them hear them. 30 And he said, Nay, father Abraham:

but if one went unto them from the dead, they will repent. 31 And he said unto him, If they hear not Moses and the prophets, neither will they be persuaded, though one rose from the dead.

Luke 16:19-31

Make a decision that while you are still alive you make peace with your creator.

THERE ARE THREE SIMPLE STEPS TO PLANNING THAT CAN BE FOLLOWED:

1) **Ascertain your location** – find out your present location or position in order to plot and navigate to your expected destination.

Example:
- How old are you now? This will help you to know whether you are on time or behind schedule.
- How rich are you now?
- What source or sources of income do you have in your life?
- What potential income sources are at your disposal?
- Do you presently have investment mentality or

financial intelligence? For example, savings, bonds, shares, equity, livestock, real estate etc.

- How poor are you now? Be honest with yourself.
- Are you in debts now? Not all debt is bad, so place yourself where you fall.
- How is your relationship with God? Prayer life, studying of the word, spending quality time in his presence, paying tithes, giving offering and sowing seeds, etc.

2) **Determine your destination** – if you don't know where you are going you won't know when you get there, that is if ever you get there. Determining your destination before commencing a journey is a normal thing for every sane person to do. How can you arrive at a destination you don't know? This is commonly referred to as having a vision.

Where there is no vision, the people perish: but he that keepeth the law, happy is he.

Proverbs 29:18

Why do we need a vision?

2 And the Lord answered me, and said, Write the vision, and make it plain upon tables, that

he may run that readeth it.3 For the vision is yet for an appointed time but at the end it shall speak, and not lie: though it tarry, wait for it; because it will surely come, it will not tarry.

Habbakuk 2:2-3

We have to write down our vision and run with it; this is a very crucial part of planning. The scripture says a vision is for an appointed time and at the end it will speak and it will not lie.

So establish the following:
- When do you want to retire or gain financial freedom or independence?
- How old do you want to be when this happens?
- How much will you need in order to take care of yourself and your obligations or responsibilities (family) when you reach the *evening* of your life?
- How rich and comfortable do you want to be by the time you reach your evening stage?

A certain research[1] has shown that when hundred young men aged twenty years are followed for forty

---

[1]By Olumide O. Emmanuel (2008) "The Pathway to Wealth". Common Sense Publishing, Lagos, Nigeria.

years till they reach sixty years, anywhere in the world, the following discoveries will be made;

- 1% of them will have attained financial independence and extremely rich and or wealthy
- 4% of them will be just rich
- 5% of them will still be working and struggling to make ends meet
- 36% of them will have died
- 54% will be broke, poor and dependent on relatives, their children, government or church welfare.

Please note that all these are destinations that we can arrive at, but the choice is yours.

I call heaven and earth to record this day against you, that I have set before you life and death, blessing and cursing: therefore choose life, that both thou and thy seed may live.

Deuteronomy 30:19

God encourages us to choose well.

3) **Choose your vehicle** – A strategy or type of

investment you choose to undertake will determine how quick you arrive at your destination.

Just like in the natural there are different modes of transportation e.g. walking, cycling, motor bike, train, car, truck, ship, airplane, jet, etc

The mode of transportation you choose will determine how quick you arrive at your destination.

Example;
- Being employed is a mode of transport to your future
- Investing in the capital market/stock market, and the like, is another level
- Real estate; buying land, building complexes, houses, etc. is another mode; they say real estate is real investment.
- Starting your own business; God said he will bless the work of your hands.
- Intellectual property; using your brain to make a living.

4) **Budgeting** – There is what is called the 70/30 principle of budgeting.

30% of your income does not belong to you;
- 10% is a tithe for God
- 10% for savings (if you don't save you are not safe)
- 10% personal development, e.g. buy a book, take a short course, etc.

70% you can live on it, including giving your offerings, helping the poor, supporting missions, and personal indulgences.

You must be disciplined to stick to your plan without distraction. You must rise above the need to please people. If you don't plan your life, people and circumstances will plan your life for you.

Finally, without a plan in place there will be poverty in place.

Chapter 2

ACT UPON YOUR CONVICTION

According to the story outlined in the ancient book, what Abraham set off to do, he went all the way to fulfil it. Many people don't achieve anything in life because they have many plans which are not acted upon. What separates ordinary people from achievers or great people in life is that they may both have plans or have dreams to do something, but the achievers rather go all the way to start acting on their plans, dreams and visions.

And Abraham rose up early in the morning, and saddled his ass, and took two of his young men with him, and Isaac his son, and clave the wood for the burnt offering, and rose up, and went unto the place of which

God had told him.

Genesis 22:3

There are people who want to go to school, they only talk about it but they do nothing about it. Others talk about starting a business, others about praying, others about being faithful to their spouses, others about tithing, and others about living holy lives in general but the major problem is the action dimension to their desires.

Abraham did not just talk about what God had laid in his heart but he acted upon it. In fact, in the spirit he went all the way to kill the boy because he had already purposed it in his heart that the boy will be offered as a burnt offering according to the instructions of God.

And Abraham stretched forth his hand, and took the knife to slay his son. 11 And the angel of the LORD called unto him out of heaven, and said, Abraham, Abraham: and he said, Here *am* I. 12 And he said, Lay not thine hand upon the lad, neither do thou anything unto him: for now I

know that thou fearest God, seeing thou hast not withheld thy son, thine only *son* from me.

Genesis 22:10-12

God demands action from our side before the supernatural can be released into our lives and or our circumstances. Just as Abraham took action to sacrifice his son and the Lord provided supernaturally a sacrifice for himself. If he could not have acted upon his convictions he would have never seen the hand of God in the way that he did.

Draw nigh to God, and he will draw nigh to you. Cleanse your hands, yee sinners; and purify your hearts, ye double minded.

James 4:8

Notice here that God wants you to make the first move and he will join in. You can never move the hand of God into your situation while you sit there and make excuses. Make a move and see how heaven will move to back you up.

At the Jordan, God said to Joshua, the soles of the feet of the priests must first touch the water and then a miracle of parting the Jordan will take place.

And it shall come to pass, as soon as the soles of the feet of the priests that bear the ark of the Lord, the Lord of all the earth, shall rest in the waters of Jordan, that the waters of Jordan shall be cut off from the waters that come down from above; and they shall stand upon an heap.

Joshua 3:13

This clearly shows to us that God expects us to live by faith and faith is never faith until you act on it.

Even Peter acted upon his convictions and saw the glory of God when he prayed for Dorcas and restored her back to life. If Peter could have never acted, this powerful miracle would have never happened.

36 In Joppa there was a disciple named Tabitha, which is translated Dorcas. She was always doing good works and acts of charity...........
39 Then Peter arose and went with them. When he was come, they brought him into the upper chamber: and all the widows stood by him weeping and shewing the coats and

garments which Dorcas made, while she was with them. 40 But Peter put them all forth, and kneeled down and prayed; and turning him to the body said Tabitha arise. And she opened her eyes: and when she saw Peter, she sat up.

Acts 9:36, 39-40

Elisha also acted and saw the hand of God. He closed himself in the room and started praying and making a demand on God to raise up the son of the Shunamite woman. When he took this step of acting by faith the power of God was released over the situation and the boy was restored back to life. He didn't just look at the child and wish for something to happen but he started doing something to provoke God for a miracle. The big question is what are you doing?

And when Elisha was come into the house, behold, the child was dead, *and* laid upon his bed. He went in therefore, and shut the door upon them twain, and prayed unto the LORD. And he went up, and lay upon the child, and put his mouth upon his mouth, and his eyes upon his eyes, and his hands upon his hands: and he stretched himself upon the child; and

the flesh of the child waxed warm. Then he returned, and walked in the house to and fro; and went up, and stretched himself upon him: and the child sneezed seven times, and the child opened his eyes.

2 Kings 4:32-35

Great things happen to people who make things happen. I have never seen or heard of any successful person who just woke up one day and they were successful without doing anything, never. If Abraham had not acted upon his convictions he may never have encountered God as Yawehjireh which means Yaweh will see and he will provide. Note that man's extremity is God's opportunity.

And he said, lay not thine hand upon the lad, neither do thou anything unto him: for now I know that thou fearest God, seeing thou hast not withheld thy son, thine only *son* from me. 13 And Abraham lifted up his eyes, and looked, and behold behind *him* a ram caught in a thicket by his horns: and Abraham went and took the ram, and offered him up for a burnt offering in the stead of his son. 14 And Abraham called the name of that place Jehovahjireh: as it is said *to*

this day, in the mount of the LORD it shall be seen.

Genesis 22:12-14

People at the top of every profession or anything they do, share one quality — *they get things done.* This ability supersedes intelligence, talent and great plans. I call it "The action habit"— the habit of putting ideas into action now — it is very essential to getting things done.

The action habit can be developed by doing the following:

1. Don't wait until conditions are perfect – If you're waiting to start when conditions are perfect, you probably will never do anything in life. There will always be something that isn't quite right; it is either the timing is off, the market is down, or there's too much competition. In the real world there is no perfect time to start. You have to take action and deal with problems as they arise. The best time to start was last year. The second best time to start is right now.

The lepers in the book of Kings demonstrated this very well. They said to one another "why sit we here until we die", this is one of the most inspiring stories in the bible. These people had every reason to just sit there and die, after all they were sick. But they didn't wait for the conditions to be perfect they just moved and the power of God assisted them along the way.

And there were four leprous men at the entering in of the gate: and they said one to another, why sit we here until we die? If we say, we will enter into the city, then the famine *is* in the city, and we shall die there: and if we sit still here, we die also. Now therefore come, and let us fall unto the host of the Syrians: if they save us alive, we shall live; and if they kill us, we shall but die. And they rose up in the twilight, to go unto the camp of the Syrians: and when they were come to the uttermost part of the camp of Syria, behold, *there was* no man there. For the Lord had made the host of the Syrians to hear a noise of chariots, and a noise of horses, *even* the noise of a great host: and they said one to another, Lo, the king of Israel hath hired against us the kings of the Hittites, and the kings of the Egyptians, to come upon us. Wherefore they arose and fled in the

twilight, and left their tents, and their horses, and their asses, even the camp as it *was*, and fled for their life. And when these lepers came to the uttermost part of the camp, they went into one tent, and did eat and drink, and carried thence silver, and gold, and raiment, and went and hid *it*; and came again, and entered into another tent, and carried thence *also*, and went and hid *it*.

2 Kings 7:3-8

The question that can be posed here is what are you waiting for? Rise up and do something, then you will also have a testimony of greatness. If God could assist the lepers with a supernatural sound, can he not assist you to realize your dreams in this lifetime? Notice that it all happened when they rose up to do something.

2. Be a doer – Practice doing things rather than just thinking about them or talking about them. Do you want to start a business? Do you want to start exercising? Do you want to buy a house? Do you want to start fasting? Do you want to start paying your tithe? Do it today. The longer an idea sits in your head without being acted on, the weaker it becomes. After a few days the details get hazy.

After some weeks it's forgotten completely. By becoming a doer you'll get more done and stimulate new ideas in the process.

> **But be ye doers of the word, and not hearers only, deceiving your own selves. For if any be a hearer of the word, and not a doer, he is like unto a man beholding his natural face in a glass: For he beholdeth himself, and goeth his way, and straightway forgetteth what manner of man he was.**
>
> **James 1:22-24**

Some people talk too much and never get to do anything. Be a doer lest you forget what manner of man you are supposed to become and God will take you far.

3. Remember that ideas alone don't bring success – Ideas are important, but they are only valuable after they have been implemented. One average idea that has been put into action is more valuable than a dozen brilliant ideas that you are saving for "some other day" or the "right opportunity" or "the right time". If you have an idea that you really believe in, do something about it now. Unless you take action it will never become anything but just a thought. If Abraham could have just thought about sacrificing his son after sometime he was going to have a million reasons why he shouldn't do it.

The soul of the sluggard desireth, and *hath* nothing: but the soul of the diligent shall be made fat.

Proverbs 13:4

4. Use action to cure fear – Have you ever noticed that the most difficult part of public speaking is waiting for your turn to speak? Even professional speakers and actors experience pre-performance anxiety. Once they get started the fear disappears. Action is the best cure for fear. The most difficult time to take action is the very first time. Once you get the ball rolling, you build confidence and things will keep getting easier. Kill fear by taking action and build on that confidence. I can never forget how I felt when God called me into ministry, I was so afraid of what was going to happen along the way, but I took a step of faith and as I kept going on, the fear factor was broken. Look at the example of Peter, he wanted to walk on water and he knew that he could easily sink but the only way to overcome that fear was to take a step of faith and start walking on water and it worked.

And when the disciples saw him walking on the sea, they were troubled, saying, It is a spirit; and they cried out for fear. But straightway Jesus spake unto them, saying, be of good cheer; it is I; be not afraid. And Peter answered him and said, Lord, if it be thou, bid me to come unto thee on the water. And he said, Come. And when Peter was come down out of the ship, he walked on the water, to go to Jesus. But when he saw the wind boisterous, he was afraid; and beginning to sink, he cried, saying, Lord, save me.

Matthew 14:26-30

Many people are concerned about the sinking of Peter but I am rather encouraged by his boldness to step out of the boat. That for me is one of the greatest miracles that Peter experienced in his lifetime which his colleagues could only wish for. For them to have had this experience they had to do what Peter did. This is what separate men from boys: Use action to cure fear.

5. Start your creative engine mechanically – One of

the biggest misconceptions about creative work is that it can only be done when inspiration strikes. If you wait for inspiration to slap you in the face, you may never do anything in life. Instead of waiting, start your creative motor mechanically. If you need to write something, force yourself to sit down and write. Put pen to paper. Brainstorm. By moving your hands you'll stimulate the flow of ideas and inspire yourself. If you knew how long it took me to start writing this book you would understand what I'm talking about. I was always saying one day I will do it, until I started my engine mechanically by creating time to seat behind the desk and start jotting down the few ideas in the pages of this book. My advice is that rise up now and begin to do something. I like how Jesus operated; he would use words like rise up and walk.

And a certain man was there, which had an infirmity thirty and eight years. When Jesus saw him lie, and knew that he had been now a long time *in that case,* he saith unto him, Wilt thou be made whole? The impotent man answered him, "Sir, I have no man, when the water is troubled, to put me into the pool: but while I am coming, another steppeth down before me." Jesus

saith unto him, "Rise, take up thy bed, and walk." And immediately the man was made whole, and took up his bed, and walked: and on the same day was the sabbath.

John 5:5-9

In this story the breakthrough of this man came about when he followed the instructions of Jesus to be mechanical about his situation. Jesus said rise up, take up thy bed and walk and it worked. Someone reading this book must rise up and start acting on some things they have been procrastinating on for a long time. Apply for school, start doing the business plan, start telling your spouse that you are sorry for what happened or that you love them, answer the call of God and start preaching the gospel, the list is endless.

I will say it again, many people have good intensions and desires but never see it become a reality due to lack of action on their part. Pursuit is the proof of desire because a heart's desire alone is not enough to produce a result. To have a good intention without acting on it is like winking at a lady in the dark and expecting her to respond. Life does not produce results by intension, but by action.

6. Live in the present – Focus on what you can do in the present moment. Don't worry about what you should have done last week or what you might be able to do tomorrow. The only time you can affect is the present. If you ruminate too much about the past or the future you won't get anything done. Tomorrow or next week frequently turns into never.

Take therefore no thought for the morrow: for the morrow shall take thought for the things of itself. Sufficient unto the day *is* the evil thereof.

Matthew 6:3-4

7. Get down to business immediately – It's common practice for people to socialize and make small talk at the beginning of meetings. The same is true for individual workers. How often do you check email or facebook before doing any real work? These distractions will cost you serious time if you don't bypass them and get down to business immediately. By becoming someone who gets to the point you'll be more productive and people will look to you as a leader.

Some people watch television just too much. Why

don't you find something more productive to do and do it immediately.

And Caleb stilled the people before Moses, and said, Let us go up at once, and possess it; for we are well able to overcome it.

Number 13:30

Great people are people who act like Caleb **"Let us go up at once, and posses it"**. What are the intentions you have that are yet to be acted upon? Get to work immediately because whatever will be, will not be; you have to make it be, and if you don't work it, it will not work.

I want to challenge you to start doing something. Many people spend all their time on the planning table of intensions and never produce fruits in the real world of action. I see you rising up to possess your dreams right now in Jesus name.

Chapter 3

A LIFE OF GREATNESS CALLS FOR SEPAR ATION

A wise man once said that where we will be in the next five years, will be determined by two things: the books we read and the friends we keep. Evil communication, no doubt, will corrupt good manners. Everybody cannot be your friend; wisdom demands that you choose your friends with care. Anybody that does not draw you closer to God or speak positively into your life must be excused from your life.

In this chapter I desire to encourage you to take inventory of those in your relational circle and ask yourself these questions: Do they add to you, multiply you, and inspire you or do they subtract from you, divide and influence you negatively? Avoid people that tolerate you instead of celebrating you. Everybody loves to be appreciated and celebrated. The human nature is packaged to thrive in a more conducive environment; an atmosphere full of love, acceptance and appreciation. When you hang around people who do not value you they will choke your potential and you will end up a commoner against the will of God for your life. No one can make you feel inferior without your permission. So even the way you treat yourself must change because it determines how other people will treat you.

It is against this background that I believe that one of the most important things that God wants us to deal with in order to prepare ourselves for greatness is the area of separation. In this chapter we learn that God instructs Abraham to go to Moriah and offer his son as a sacrifice.

And it came to pass after these things, that God did tempt Abraham, and said unto him, Abraham: and he said, Behold, *here I am*. 2 And he said, Take now thy son, thine only *son*

Isaac, whom thou lovest, and get thee into the land of Moriah; and offer him there for a burnt offering upon one of the mountains which I will tell thee of.

Genesis 22:1-2

When we set off in the journey to greatness we must always detach ourselves from our usual ordinary surroundings, from the people around us, from what's happening around us and from the things which easily disturb and distract us. We learn that God called Abraham away from his usual environment and he also left there some of the most significant relations in his life, he went with the people that he understood could easily take instructions from him and not interfere with where God wanted to take him. Even these particular people that he went with at a certain point he told them to remain behind with the donkeys as he went yonder to worship the Lord with his son.

And Abraham said unto his young men, Abide ye here with the ass; and I and the lad will go yonder and worship, and come again to you.

Genesis 22:5

I want to believe that Abraham understood that

these people were most likely to stop him to achieve his intended purpose as he had agreed with God. I cannot imagine them just watching him take the knife to kill his son; they were most likely going to try and stop him or convince him to do it differently from the way God had instructed him. This is very key because when you hang around non-dreamers they may want to discourage you from running with your vision. Sometimes they can start asking you questions so that they discourage you. Where are you going to get money from? They might even remind you that nobody has ever done what you intend to do. Some will tell you not in this country may be if you were in Europe or if you were a child of so and so. Look you don't need such people in your life let them remain with donkeys while you continue to achieve what is burning in your heart.

Jesus was faced with a similar situation at one point in his life. Peter wanted to stop him from going to the cross, Jesus was not impressed with this shenanigan and told Peter to get behind him and He even called Peter Satan. In fact, anyone that discourages you from doing the will of God in your life is more often than not, being influenced by Satan.

From that time forth began Jesus to shew unto his disciples, how that he must go unto Jerusalem, and suffer many things of the elders and chief priests and scribes, and be killed, and be raised again the third day. Then Peter took him, and began to rebuke him, saying, be it far from thee, Lord: this shall not be unto thee. But he turned, and said unto Peter, Get thee behind me, Satan: thou art an offence unto me: for thou savourest not the things that be of God, but those that be of men.

Matthew 16:21-23

You can realize from the above text that having certain people around you when you want to embark on a life changing journey can be very unfruitful. The truth is that those people will not be hearing what God is whispering in your spirit. The dream you are carrying is sometimes too big for others to comprehend; this is why separation becomes crucial if you really want to go far in life.

Separation is a place where destinies are decided, it was through this separation that Jesus arrived at a place of willingness to lay down his life for humanity. At this time, we realize that having certain people in your life can hinder you to do the will of God for your life.

Joseph was a dreamer and his brothers didn't understand him. This went to the extent that they even planned to kill him. They wanted to kill the dream that he had but God used one of them to preserve his life and they sold him to some passer-byes. I believe God was separating Joseph from his brothers because they were going to hinder him from realizing his dream.

> **Come, and let us sell him to the Ishmeelites, and let not our hand be upon him; for he *is* our brother *and* our flesh. And his brethren were content. 28 Then there passed by Midianites merchantmen; and they drew and lifted up Joseph out of the pit, and sold Joseph to the Ishmeelites for twenty *pieces* of silver: and they brought Joseph into Egypt.**
>
> **Genesis 37:27-28**

Many years later after Joseph had been separated from his brothers his dream became a reality.

And Pharaoh said unto his servants, can we find *such one* as this *is,* a man in whom the Spirit of God *is?* 39And Pharaoh said unto Joseph, Forasmuch as God hath shewed thee all this, *there is* none so discreet and wise as thou *art:* 40 Thou shalt be over my house, and according unto thy word shall all my people be ruled: only in the throne will I be greater than thou. 41 And Pharaoh said unto Joseph, See, I have set thee over all the land of Egypt.

Genesis 41:38- 41

A little over seven years after this, Joseph's brothers came into Egypt looking for food and they had to bow before Joseph because he was a great man. His dream got fulfilled right in their eyes.

And Joseph *was* the governor over the land, *and* he *it was* that sold to all the people of the land: and Joseph's brethren came, and bowed down
themselves before him *with* their faces to the earth.

Genesis 42:6

Note that it took separation in order for Joseph to

realize his dream. Later on, his own father came and bowed down with his brethren according to the dream that Joseph had. This dream might never have come to pass if Joseph had continued living among his brethren.

Peter also separated from the crowd to raise Dorcas from the dead.

> **Then Peter arose and went with them. When he was come, they brought him into the upper chamber: and all the widows stood by him weeping and shewing the coats and garments which Dorcas made, while she was with them. But Peter put them all forth, and kneeled down, and prayed; and turning *him* to the body said, Tabitha, arise. And she opened her eyes: and when she saw Peter, she sat up. And he gave her *his* hand, and lifted her up, and when he had called the saints and widows, presented her alive.**
>
> **Acts 9:39-41**

Jesus separated from the mourners to raise the little girl at Jabirus' house.

And he cometh to the house of the ruler of the synagogue, and seeth the tumult, and them that wept and wailed greatly. And when he was come in, he saith unto them, why make ye this ado, and weep? The damsel is not dead, but sleepeth. And they laughed him to scorn. But when he had put them all out, he taketh the father and the mother of the damsel, and them that were with him, and entereth in where the damsel was lying. And he took the damsel by the hand, and said unto her, Talithacumi; which is, being interpreted, Damsel, I say unto thee, arise. And straightway the damsel arose, and walked; for she was *of the age* of twelve years. And they were astonished with a great astonishment.

Mark 5:38-42

Jacob separated from the rest of the people and he had an encounter with God. His true identity was revealed to him when he was on his own. It was during this encounter that he learned for the first time that his true name was Israel. The amazing thing is that while he was in the crowd he couldn't encounter God in this way that changed his life forever.

And he rose up that night, and took his two wives, and his two women servants, and his eleven sons, and passed over the ford Jabbok. And he took them, and sent them over the brook, and sent over that he had. And Jacob was left alone; and there wrestled a man with him until the breaking of the day.

Genesis 32:22-24

I reckon you now notice this principle of separation is all over the bible, if you want to do something of significance in this life separate yourself, and you will be heading in the right direction to becoming great.

The bible has this to say about wrong associations;

Be not deceived: evil communications corrupt good manners.

1 Corinthians 15:33

At least you must identify people who have a similar dream and or passion and hook up with them if you need assistance but most of the times these type of people are very rare to find.

He that walketh with wise *men* shall be wise: but a companion of fools shall be destroyed.
Proverbs 13:20

So Abraham had to leave his usual geographical location to avoid familiarity; his wife to avoid emotional attachments and the servants to avoid interruption.

You may have to look into your life and make necessary adjustments as far as separation is concerned. If you want to go far in life and realise the greatness that God has deposited inside of you, choose your friends well. Sometimes it is your friends who are not living holy lives; it could also mean separation from being involved in corruption, wrong relationships such as extramarital affairs. Separation could even mean stopping to go to certain places like beer halls or churches that do not preach the Spirit-filled truth of the word of God. The interesting thing about this issue of separation is that you know for sure what is preventing you from going far in life, why don't you just let go and let God. It could even be issues of attitude; nobody can advise you or you can't even keep relationships because of a stinking attitude or a big mouth. Whatever it is, let go and let God take over your life.

This same Abraham, God instructed him to leave his own people and a country where he grew up in order for him to experience the great plans that God had for his life.

Now the LORD had said unto Abram, Get thee out of thy country, and from thy kindred, and from thy father's house, unto a land that I will shew thee: 2 And I will make of thee a great nation, and I will bless thee, and make thy name great; and thou shalt be a blessing: 3 And I will bless them that bless thee, and curse him that curseth thee: and in thee shall all families of the earth be blessed. 4So Abram departed, as the LORD had spoken unto him; and Lot went with him: and Abram *was* seventy and five years old when he departed out of Haran.

Genesis 12:1-4

It is very clear that God didn't want to do what he wanted to do in the life of Abram while he was still in Haran. There could have been things or people in this place that God knew might distract Abram from walking into the greatness that he intended for him.

And just like many of us when Abram left his country he took along him someone from that place and this also further delayed the plan of God for his life.

And Abram took Sarai his wife, and Lot his brother's son, and all their substance that they had gathered, and the souls that they had gotten in Haran; and they went forth to go into the land of Canaan; and into the land of Canaan they came.

Genesis 12:5

You know, sometimes in life we have things that we like that are very useless to us as far as our destinies are concerned. Many times we cling to them and they become the reason why we never go far in life. This nephew of Abram, called Lot, became a problem on the way and the plans of God were being delayed.

And Lot also, which went with Abram, had flocks, and herds, and tents. 6 And the land was not able to bear them, that they might dwell together: for their substance was great, so that they could not dwell together. 7 And there was strife between the herd men of

Abram's cattle and the herdmen of Lot's cattle: and the Canaanite and the Perizzite dwelled then in the land. 8 And Abram said unto Lot, Let there be no strife, I pray thee, between me and thee, and between my herdmen and thy herdmen; for we *be* brethren. 9 *Is* not the whole land before thee? Separate thyself, I pray thee, from me: if *thou wilt take* the left hand, then I will go to the right; or if *thou depart* to the right hand, then I will go to the left. 10 And Lot lifted up his eyes, and beheld all the plain of Jordan, that it *was* well watered everywhere, before the LORD destroyed Sodom and Gomorrah, *even* as the garden of the LORD, like the land of Egypt, as thou comest unto Zoar. 11 Then Lot chose him all the plain of Jordan; and Lot journeyed east: and they separated themselves the one from the other. 12 Abram dwelled in the land of Canaan, and Lot dwelled in the cities of the plain, and pitched *his* tent toward Sodom.

Genesis 13:5-12

It was just after Lot left the life of Abraham that the Lord spoke to him again to reveal His intentions.

And the LORD said unto Abram, after that Lot was separated from him, lift up now thine eyes, and look from the place where thou art northward, and southward, and eastward, and westward: 15 For all the land which thou seest, to thee will I give it, and to thy seed forever.16 And I will make thy seed as the dust of the earth: so that if a man can number the dust of the earth, *then* shall thy seed also be numbered. 17 Arise, walk through the land in the length of it and in the breadth of it; for I will give it unto thee. 18 Then Abram removed *his* tent, and came and dwelt in the plain of Mamre, which *is* in Hebron, and built there an altar unto the LORD.

Genesis 13:14-18

Someone reading this book the Lord is waiting for you to separate from Lot and the next instruction for your life will come. You can't walk into greatness with Lot by your side; he is only with you to delay your destiny. Let go of Lot and you will begin to see great things in your life. It is very clear here that Lot was a hindrance because the bible says **"And the LORD said unto Abram, after Lot was separated from him..."** Could it be that the next level of your life is hidden in your separation with certain people or certain habits that are pulling you back? Rise up and make the necessary adjustments in your life and you will begin to see clearly where you are going in Jesus name.

Chapter 4

THE POWER OF THE TONGUE
(ANNOUNCE YOUR INTENTIONS BY FAITH)

You can never rise above your confession. Many people don't go far in life because they don't understand the power of words. If you don't understand the power of words you can use them loosely only to realise that you have been snared, crippled and limited by your own words. I have been tremendously blessed here by the way Abraham communicates to his servants; it opens up one of the treasures that we need to discover in order for us to go far in this journey of life. Just read this verse, it is so powerful.

And Abraham said unto his young men, Abide ye here with the ass; and I and the lad will go yonder and worship, and come again to you.

Genesis 22:5

Part "b" of that verse is amazing "...**and I and the lad will go yonder and worship, and come again to you.**" I don't know if you hear what this man is saying; he is saying "I am going to sacrifice my son; however, I believe he is not going to die and hence we are going to come back together". These are faith-filled words, though Abraham was obeying God he still believed that God will do something to spare his son. Why else would he say they are going to come back together if he didn't believe God will perform a miracle or change his mind?

The lesson here is that stop cursing yourself with words you utter because of the circumstances you find yourself in. Start speaking what you desire to happen, not what you regret to happen in your life. The bible puts it this way;

(As it is written, I have made thee a father of many nations,) before him whom he believed, *even* God, who quickeneth the

dead, and calleth those things which be not as though they were.

Romans 4:17

Even God calls those things that be not as though they were; be imitators of God. In the beginning God was faced with a situation, but the bible makes it very clear that God did not start discussing that situation but rather he began to say what he wanted.

And the earth was without form, and void; and darkness *was* upon the face of the deep. And the Spirit of God moved upon the face of the waters. And God said, Let there be light: and there was light. And God saw the light, that *it was* good: and God divided the light from the darkness.

Gen 1:4

You must understand that your tongue was given to you to determine the course of your life. The bible says;

Death and life are in the power of the tongue: and they that love it shall eat the fruit thereof.

Proverb 18:21

Meaning that you can kill your destiny with your tongue and you can bring life to your destiny with your tongue. Don't take your words lightly they are very powerful. If you can learn the art of using your tongue you can go very far in life. You can win battles and change your world through your tongue. The Apostle James has this to say about the tongue;

Now when we put bits into the mouths of horses to make them obey us, we also guide the whole animal. 4 And consider ships: Though very large and driven by fierce winds, they are guided by a very small rudder wherever the will of the pilot directs. 5 So too, though the tongue is a small part of the body, it boasts great things. Consider how large a forest a small fire ignites. 6 And the tongue is a fire, a world of unrighteousness, is placed among the parts of our bodies. It pollutes the whole body, sets the course of life on fire, and is set on fire of hell. 7 Every

sea creature, reptile, bird, or animal is tamed and has been tamed by man, 8 but no man can tame the tongue. It is a restless evil, full of deadly poison. 9 We praise our Lord and Father with it, and we curse men who are made in God's likeness with it. 10 Praising and cursing come out of the same mouth. My brothers, these things should not be this way. 11 Does a spring pour out sweet and bitter water from the same opening? 12 Can a fig tree produce olives, my brothers, or a grapevine produce figs? Neither can a salt water spring yield fresh water.

James 3:3-12

I like verse six "**And the tongue is a fire. The tongue is a**
world..." Your tongue if used properly can create your world. Just as a little fire can light and burn a forest, so can your tongue affect your entire life. If you can master your tongue you can also master your destiny.

Jesus demonstrated this very well with the fig tree.

And on the morrow, when they were come from Bethany, he was hungry: 13 And seeing

a fig tree afar off having leaves, he came, if haply he might find anything there on: and when he came to it, he found nothing but leaves; for the time of figs was not *yet*. 14And Jesus answered and said unto it, No man eat fruit of thee hereafter forever. And his disciples heard *it*.

Mark 11:12-14

His words did not fall to the ground,

And in the morning, as they passed by, they saw the fig tree dried up from the roots. And Peter calling to remembrance saith unto him, Master, behold, the fig tree which thou cursedst is withered away.

Mark 11:20-21

The fig tree withered away and all Jesus did was to speak to it and curse it.

Even when we pray it is our words which make a difference, as I was studying the prayer of Daniel I realised that the whole battle over Persia was a battle of words.

Then said he unto me, Fear not, Daniel: for from the first day that thou didst set thine heart to understand and to chasten thyself before thy God, thy words were heard, and I am come for thy words.

Daniel 10:12

Notice what the angel says to Daniel, thy words were heard and I am come for thy words, it is all about words.

The war between Goliath and David was a war of words. Goliath said and David said and Goliath said and David said.

And the Philistine said unto David, *Am* I a dog that thou comest to me with staves? And the Philistine cursed David by his gods. And the Philistine said to David, Come to me, and I will give thy flesh unto the fowls of the air, and to the beasts of the field. Then said David to the Philistine, thou comest to me with a sword, and with a spear, and with a shield: but I come to thee in the name of the LORD of hosts, the God of the armies of Israel, whom thou hast defied. This day will the LORD deliver thee into mine hand; and I will

smite thee, and take thine head from thee; and I will give the carcases of the host of the Philistines this day unto the fowls of the air, and to the wild beasts of the earth; that all the earth may know that there is a God in Israel. And all this assembly shall know that the LORD saveth not with sword and spear: for the battle *is* the LORD'S, and he will give you into our hands.

1Samuel 17:43-47

A close study at the above text will reveal to you that David's victory over Goliath started with the words he declared. Many people allow only the devil to speak to them and they don't respond to him with faith-filled words that counter attack the lies of the enemy. When Satan says they are good for nothing or they are failures or they will never amount to anything, they say amen to that rather than declaring the mind of God over their lives. Announce like David and let the enemy know that you are a child of a great God who is able to turn a nothing into something and that you are able to do all things through Christ who strengthens you.

Wise men when they had an encounter with God asked him to touch their tongues;

Then said I, Woe *is* me! For I am undone; because I *am* a man of unclean lips, and I dwell in the midst of a people of unclean lips: for mine eyes have seen the King, the LORD of hosts. 6 Then flew one of the seraphims unto me, having a live coal in his hand, *which* he had taken with the tongs from off the altar: 7 And he laid *it* upon my mouth, and said, Lo, this hath touched thy lips; and thine iniquity is taken away, and thy sin purged.

Isaiah 6:5-7

I remember a situation when God wanted to force a blessing into the life of Zacharias. He had to close his mouth because he didn't seem to want to cooperate with God, he wanted to say the wrong things meanwhile God had a plan to allow John the Baptist to be born in order for him to fulfil his eternal purposes;

But the angel said unto him, Fear not, Zacharias: for thy prayer is heard; and thy wife Elisabeth shall bear thee a son, and thou shalt call his name John.

Luke 1:13

Zacharias struggled with this because he knew the situation at home, he knew how old his wife was and how many times they had tried to have a baby when they were younger to no avail.

And Zacharias said unto the angel, whereby shall I know this? For I am an old man and my wife is well stricken in years. And the angel answering said unto him, I am Gabriel, that stand in the presence of God; and am sent to speak unto thee, and to shew thee these glad tidings. And, behold, thou shalt be dumb, and not able to speak, until the day that these things shall be performed, because thou believest not my words, which shall be fulfilled in their season.

Luke 1:18-20

Notice here that the angel says the old man had unbelief and the angel didn't want him to declare that unbelief because it would have interfered with the plan of God. This is the reason why he was made dumb.

The issue of words and the tongue is very important in the kingdom of God. No wonder God was so mindful to touch the tongues of his servants when he called them. This is what Jeremiah has to say to us about what happened when God called him;

Then the Lord reached out His hand, touched my mouth, and told me: I have now filled your mouth with my words. See, I have appointed you today over nation's and kingdoms to uproot and tear down, to destroy and demolish, to build and plant.

Jeremiah 1:9-10

Notice that the uprooting, tearing down, destroying, demolishing, building and planting was to be achieved by the words that were put in Jeremiah's mouth. What kind of words are you having in your mouth?

To Ezekiel he says;

And he said unto me, Son of man, cause thy belly to eat, and fill thy bowels with this roll that I give thee. Then did I eat *it;* and it was in my mouth as honey for sweetness.

Ezekiel 3:3

Later on God makes a demand on what he ate. Watch this;

The hand of the LORD was upon me, and carried me out in the spirit of the LORD, and set me down in the midst of the valley which *was* full of bones, And caused me to pass by them round about: and, behold, *there were* very many in the open valley; and, lo, *they were* very dry. And he said unto me, Son of man, can these bones live? And I answered, O Lord GOD, thou knowest. Again he said unto me, Prophesy upon these bones, and say unto them, O ye dry bones, hear the word of the LORD.

Ezekiel 37:1-4

God told Ezekiel to eat the word because he wanted to affect his speech, He wanted to give him words of life and later on He says to him can this dead, hopeless situation be changed, He gives him the answer right there to prophesy or announce the intended purposes of God on the situation by saying his words. God makes it very clear that it is by speaking that a situation can be turned around **"...and say unto them, O ye dry bones, hear the**

word of the LORD." What are you saying about yourself, your children, your marriage, your business, your ministry, your future? Just say what you desire not what you see and it shall be well with you in Jesus name.

Speaking the word of God over situations is very powerful. The word of God is very powerful and can change any situation if spoken but faith.

> *Is* **not my word like as a fire? saith the LORD; and like a hammer** *that* **breaketh the rock in pieces?**
>
> **Jeremiah 23:29**

As you speak the word of God over your life it destroys anything that is not of God in your life. Anything standing on your way to disturb your future can be destroyed by the word of God. Declare the word of God over that limitation and it shall catch fire in Jesus name.

Jesus makes us aware about the nature of the word;

It is the spirit that quickeneth; the flesh profiteth nothing: the words that I speak unto you, *they* are spirit, and *they* are life.

John 6:63

When a believer speaks the word of God over any circumstance the power of God is released.

While Peter yet spake these words, the Holy Ghost fell on all them which heard the word.

Act 10:44

As you declare your desires and your dreams, the spirit of God is entering your destiny in Jesus name. Understand that your tongue has creative power.

And the spirit entered into me when he spake unto me, and set me upon my feet, that I heard him that spake unto me.

Ezekiel 2:2

Notice here that the spirit entered into him when God spoke to him. This means that words carry a certain spirit behind them, whether it is the spirit of God or the spirit of the enemy. This is the spirit that brings life or destroys dreams. As you embark on this journey you must master your tongue, don't just speak anything anyhow; speak strategically so that your life will follow the direction of your words.

3 Now when we put bits into the mouths of horses to make them obey us, we also guide the whole animal. 4 And consider ships: Though very large and driven by fierce winds, they are guided by a very small rudder wherever the will of the pilot directs. 5 So too, though the tongue is a small part of the body, it boasts great things. Consider how large a forest a small fire ignites. 6 And the tongue is a fire, a world of unrighteousness, is placed among the parts of our bodies. It pollutes the whole body, sets the course of life on fire, and is set on fire of hell. 7 Every sea creature, reptile, bird, or animal is tamed and has been tamed by man, 8 but no man can tame the tongue. It is a restless evil, full of deadly poison. 9 We praise our Lord and Father with it, and we curse men who are made in God's likeness with it. 10 Praising and cursing come out of the same mouth. My brothers, these things should not be this way. 11 Does a spring pour out sweet and bitter water from the same opening? 12 Can a fig tree produce olives, my brothers, or a grapevine produce figs? Neither can a salt water spring yield fresh water.

James 3:3-12

Chapter 5

BE EQUIPPED FOR THE JOURNEY

Many times when the word 'preparation' is mentioned, our minds immediately start thinking of academic preparations. Taking a course to study something in line with what one wants to achieve ant that is good; we need to do that in order for us to sharpen our skills.

If the iron be blunt, and he do not whet the edge, then must he put to more strength: but wisdom is profitable to direct.

Ecclesiastes 10:10

However, in this chapter, I want us to look at preparation in terms of other practical virtues that are needed in the journey to greatness which are also of equal importance if we are to arrive at our desired destinations.

Abraham was equipped for the journey.

And Abraham took the wood of the burnt offering, and laid it upon Isaac his son; and he took the fire in his hand, and a knife; and they went both of them together.

Genesis 22:6

In this text we learn that as Abraham was going on his journey, he took everything he needed in order to fulfil his assignment. He took some items that were going to be useful for the assignment. The bible says he took the wood, the fire, the knife and the sacrifice. In this chapter, I want to discuss these items revelationally, and I believe this revelation will encourage you to reach your highest potential in life.

1. The wood – I want to use the wood here to represent the testimony in your life. Wood comes from a dead plant and I want to believe that wood speaks of something that is dead, something you have killed or overcome in your lifetime. What have you conquered? Recalling the victories that you have had in your past life has a way of injecting fuel into your system to try again and reach forward despite the challenges you might be facing now. Rehearsing past victories sort of reminds you that God is able to help you achieve great things in your life.

34. And David said unto Saul, Thy servant kept his father's sheep, and there came a lion, and a bear, and took a lamb out of the flock: ... 36. Thy servant slew both the lion and the bear: and this uncircumcised Philistine shall be as one of them, seeing he hath defied the armies of the living God.

1 Samuel 17:34 &36

David's confidence was fuelled by the fact that he had conquered something in the past. Never forget where God has taken you from and what he brought you through. Many people tremble in the face of adversity simple because they forget the faithfulness of God and what he has been able to do for them in the past. Oh I love David; he is able to encourage himself in the Lord, using his past victories. I can hear you saying "I prepared for this and that and it became successful and I trust that the Lord will give me grace to overcome this project I am starting also." This attitude is very critical in our lives if we are to continue our journey to greatness. The truth of the matter is that it is not always going to be easy and we are bound to meet opposition along the way and should be able to speak like David and say **"Thy servant slew both the lion and the bear: and this uncircumcised Philistine shall be as one of them"**.

The power to kill what you are facing comes from the rehearsal of your past victories commonly referred to as a testimony.

And they overcame him by the Blood of the Lamb, and by the word of their testimony; and they did loved not their lives unto death.
Revelation 12:11

2. The fire– I want to discuss the fire here to represent passion or zeal. Many people do not go anywhere in life because they are not passionate about what they want to achieve. How convinced are you about what you want to attain or achieve? Do you have the fire of passion in your heart and your spirit? How passionate are you about what you want to achieve? How hungry are you for your dream? How much do you want to achieve what you are attempting to do? These and many related questions will help you establish in your heart how much you need the results of what you are anticipating to do. The following verses will illustrate for you, the power of zeal or passion in your life with regard to the things you desire to do.

Looking unto Jesus the author and finisher of our faith; who for the JOY that was set before him endured the cross, despising the shame, and is set down at the right hand of the throne of God.

Hebrews 12:2

Jesus was very passionate about our salvation and this made him to despise the shame of the cross. There was a joy he was looking at, on the other side of the cross; the joy of having brothers who will call his Father their father. Our saviour and Lord was very passionate about this and nothing was going to stand on his way even death on the cross.

Of the increase of his government and peace there shall be no end, upon the throne of

David, and upon his kingdom, to order it, and to establish it with judgment and with justice from henceforth even forever. The ZEAL of the Lord of hosts will perform this.

Isaiah 9:7

The zeal of the Lord can perform certain things in our lives that we could never have thought possible. You can employ zeal or passion and you will see great results in your life; for the zeal of the Lord shall perform it for you in Jesus name.

For out of Jerusalem shall go forth a remnant, and they that escape out of mount Zion: the zeal of the Lord of hosts shall do this.

Isaiah 37:32

Zeal is able to do things or perform certain things that can otherwise not be performed. Do you want it so bad that you are willing to die for it? Then go for it and see the power of zeal or passion carry you through. I'm not implying by any means that it will be easy but the truth is if you want it so bad nothing can stand on your way. I remember when the Lord called me into ministry, it was not an easy thing, but the strong desire to obey the call birthed a passion in me and to be honest sometimes I look back and wonder how I managed to pull through. God is very faithful; his zeal shall do what you never thought possible.

3. Knife– A knife is designed to cut. As you go on the journey to be great, you should be prepared to receive correction from God or you should have the heart of repentance. This is the part that many people don't want to hear about. Not many people like to be corrected. When they are corrected they pick offense. The following verses of scriptures emphasises the need to leave room for correction to be ministered to us.

> **While it is said, today if ye will hear his voice, harden not your hearts, as in the provocation (rebellion).....**
>
> **AMP. Hebrews 3:15**

> **One who becomes stiff necked, after many reprimands will be shattered instantly — beyond recovery.**
>
> **HCSB. Proverbs 29:1**

If you can't be corrected you can't go far in life. In fact the bible here says you will be shattered, meaning that a person who cannot receive correction, never amounts to anything. We all need mentors in our lives, you need someone who you can be accountable to in life and when you are shown that the decisions you are about to take are wrong, listen and act accordingly.

Where no counsel is, the people fall, but in the multitude of counselors there is safety.

Proverbs 11:14

Certain habits must be allowed to die in our lives. There are certain altitudes that you can't reach with certain attitudes, characters and habits. To achieve greatness the Lord's way, you must be prepared to change in all areas of your life where there is need.

In the year that king Uzziah died I saw also the Lord sitting upon a throne, high and lifted up, and his train filled the temple.

Isaiah 6:1

When certain habits die in our lives we are able to enter into higher dimensions of success. It is very interesting here that when King Uzziah died, who is said to have been the uncle to the prophet Isaiah, instead of the prophet to fall into depression, his spiritual senses were rather energized, and he began to see God in a way that he had never seen him before. Uzziah was a good man but to the latter days of his kingship, pride entered his heart and he thought he could replace the priesthood which was ordained by God. The following verses will give you insight into the kind of sin that cost King Uzziah his life and the hindrance he was in the house of God, because of his sinful lifestyle.

17 And Azariah the priest went in after him, and with him fourscore priests of the LORD, *that were* **valiant men: 18 And they withstood Uzziah the king, and said unto him,** *It appertaineth* **not unto thee, Uzziah, to burn incense unto the LORD, but to the priests the sons of Aaron, that are consecrated to burning cense: go out of the sanctuary; for thou has trespassed; neither** *shall it be* **for thine honour from the LORD God. 19 Then Uzziah was wroth, and** *had* **a censer in his hand to burn incense: and while he was wroth with the priests, the leprosy even rose up in his forehead before the priests in the house of the LORD, from beside the incense altar. 20 And Azariah the chief priest, and all the priests, looked upon him, and, behold, he** *was* **leprous in his forehead, and they thrust**

him out from thence; yea, himself hasted also to go out, because the LORD had smitten him. 21 And Uzziah the king was a leper unto the day of his death, and dwelt in a several house, *being* a leper; for he was cut off from the house of the LORD: and Jotham his son *was* over the king's house, judging the people of the land. 22 Now the rest of the acts of Uzziah, first and last, did Isaiah the prophet, the son of Amoz, write. 23 So Uzziah slept with his fathers, and they buried him with his fathers in the field of the burial which *belonged* to the kings; for they said, He *is* a leper: and Jotham his son reigned in his stead.

2Chronicles 26:17-23

People like King Uzziah never go too far in life, their dreams and wishes die at a very early stage of their lives. Please be a person that repents when you are shown your short comings; don't be like king Uzziah who refused counsel from the priests. In this journey to greatness we must carry the knife which is the readiness of our hearts to be circumcised or to repent when we have sinned against God.

4. Sacrifice– It is very advisable that as you go on

the journey to greatness you must have a pledge as to what you will do for the Lord if he blesses you, or if he helps you to achieve your dreams. Many of us forget to thank God with our substance after the Lord has brought us to a place of greatness and success. Jacob made a pledge to God before he had anything or even achieved anything in his life, all he had was a dream, nothing more, but even at that time he made a vow to the Lord.

And this stone, which I have set for a pillar, shall be God's house: and of all that thou shalt give me I will surely give the tenth unto thee.

Genesis 28:22

I believe when God sees our willingness to partner with him and build his kingdom, there is a certain dimension of favour that he allows us to walk in.

In the book of Samuel, Hannah broke the power of bareness by fasting and prayer. Hannah's prayer was not an ordinary prayer, the following verse says as she prayed she made a vow that whatever God would give her, she would give it back to Him.

And she vowed a vow, and said, O LORD of hosts, if thou wilt indeed look on the affliction of thine handmaid, and remember me, and not forget thine handmaid, but wilt give unto thine handmaid a man child, then I will give him unto the LORD all the days of his life, and there shall no razor come upon his head.

1Samuel 1:11

Wow! My conviction is that God will never forsake these kind of people without assisting them and blessing them and making sure that their dreams come to pass. After Hannah did what she promised God, the bible has this to say about her.

And the LORD visited Hannah, so that she conceived, and bare three sons and two daughters. And the child Samuel grew before the LORD.

1Samuel 2:21

A woman who was barren suddenly became the talk of the city as the Lord blessed her for the sacrifice that she made for God by offering her only child to serve in the house of God.

In conclusion of this chapter, I want to remind you

that Abraham took the fire, the wood, the knife and the sacrifice as he was going in the direction of where God was taking him. He was well prepared for the journey. How prepared are you to go to a higher dimension of your life. I like it when the bible reveals to us that God believes that people must be prepared for the journey ahead of them.

7 And the angel of the LORD came again the second time, and touched him, and said, Arise *and* eat; because the journey *is* too great for thee. 8 And he arose, and did eat and drink, and went in the strength of that meat forty days and forty nights unto Horeb the mount of God.

1Kings 19:7-8

God knew that Elijah is going to need strength so he sent an angel to give him supernatural bread so that he can make the journey with ease. Preparation is very critical if we are to make it in this journey of success. Often time's people take off without the necessary tools of doing the work that God is calling them to do. Yes you have to be well-equipped for the journey yourself. I know you are ready to act upon your convictions but are you equipped for the journey?

Then the Lord put forth his hand, and touched my mouth, and the Lord said unto me, Behold, I have put my words in thy mouth.

Jeremiah 1:9

God said to Jeremiah "I have ordained you a prophet"; also notice he says "but I have put my words in your mouth to speak." In other words, God was saying 'you are equipped for the assignment for which I'm calling you for.'

And, being assembled together with them, commanded them that they should not depart from Jerusalem, but wait for the promise of the Father, which, saith he, ye have heard of me.

Acts 1:4

We deduce, from the above scripture, that it will be suicidal for the disciples to go into the field of the work of ministry without being equipped with the anointing of the Holy Spirit.

I pray that God will open your eyes to understand the power of preparation in any assignment you embark on in life. If you can prepare well you will make it in this life. I see you going to your place of greatness in Jesus name.

Chapter 6

THE FEAR OF THE LORD

Obeying God requires the fear of God in our lives. If Abraham did not have the fear of the Lord he could easily have dismissed the instructions that God was giving him. He knew that God had the power to give and to take what he has given him, so he decided that whatever God required from his life he would not withhold. The story of Jonah illustrates this very well.

6 And the LORD God prepared a gourd, and made *it* to come up over Jonah, that it might be

a shadow over his head, to deliver him from his grief. So Jonah was exceeding glad of the gourd. 7 But God prepared a worm when the morning rose the next day, and it smote the gourd that it withered.

Jonah 4:6-7

Notice here that the same God that created the tree for Jonah to give him a shade is the same God that sent the worm to devour it. This teaches us that on our journey to greatness God is the giver of talents and abilities and He can just as easily take it all away; thus the fear of God remains paramount. There are people who when they start succeeding they start thinking that they are the ones who earned their success through their intelligence and or their hard work. But the bible has this to say to that effect.

But thou shalt remember the LORD thy God: for *it is* he that giveth thee power to get wealth, that he may establish his covenant which he sware unto thy fathers, as *it is* this day.

Deuteronomy 8:18

The fear of God will protect you against vain glory. The fear of the Lord will help you to remain humble at all times. There are people who start well in life but end up being destroyed because along the way they forget God. But the word of God is full of Godly instructions that caution us against such things.

The fear of the Lord is the beginning of knowledge: but fools despise wisdom and instruction.

Proverbs 1:7

And now, Israel, what doth the Lord thy God require of thee, but to fear the Lord thy God, to walk in all his ways, and to love him, and to serve the Lord thy God with all thy heart and with all thy soul...

Deuteronomy 10:12

If ye will fear the Lord, and serve him, and obey his voice, and not rebel against the commandment of the Lord, then shall both ye and also the king that reigneth over you continue following the Lord your God.

1 Samuel 12:14

For in the multitude of dreams and many words there are also diverse vanities: but fear

thou God.

Ecclesiastes 5:7

There are people who like explaining too much, and their explanation does not lead to the righteousness of God, all they are saying is to try and defend their lifestyles which are not pleasing to God.

Let us hear the conclusion of the whole matter: Fear God, and keep his commandments: for this is the whole duty of man.

Ecclesiastes 12:13

Even the way we relate in the marital home; the bible encourages us that as we live together, the fear of God must be found in our lives. This is why you cannot disrespect your spouse either by insults, calling them names or any such things because you are living together in the fear of God. We ought to submit and be humble to one another.

Submitting yourselves one to another in the fear of God.

Ephesians 5:21

Though a sinner do evil an hundred times and his days be prolonged, yet surely I know that it shall be well with them that fear God, which fear before him.

Ecclesiastes 8:12

So living long is not always a justification that God is happy with you, the main thing is to fear God. It is the whole duty of man. The fear of God is the only true mark of greatness that God endorses. It is very possible that sometimes we may appear to be great in our own eyes while in the eyes of God we are failures because of the lack of the fear of God.

And fear came upon every soul: and many wonders and signs were done by the apostles.

Acts 2:43

Even miracles require the environment of the fear of God in order for them to happen. Where the fear of God is absent God cannot do great works, and this includes even in your very life. Whatever you are doing let God be God in your life and your success will be a good success.

This book of the law shall not depart out of thy mouth; but thou shalt meditate therein day and night, that thou mayest observe to do according to all that is written therein: for then thou shalt make thy way prosperous, and then thou shalt have good success.

Joshua 1:8

The verse we have just read makes us aware that there is a good success and if there is a good success then there is bad success. I believe bad success is the one that God is not glorified in. May the Lord help us to achieve good success in Jesus name.

Chapter 7

WINNING PRAYER THAT MAKES ME GR EAT

And Abraham said unto his young men, abide ye here with the ass; and I and the lad will go yonder and worship, and come again to you.

Genesis 22:5

The words used in this verse **"to worship"** denotes that
Abraham was going up the mountain to pray. This is because worship is a type of prayer. Another very

critical area that we all must explore on the journey to greatness is the area of having a prayerful lifestyle. The following scripture shows us the importance of prayer.

14 If my people, which are called by my name, shall humble themselves, and pray, and seek my face, and turn from their wicked ways; then will I hear from heaven, and will forgive their sin, and will heal their land. 15 Now mine eyes shall be open, and mine ears attent unto the prayer *that is made* in this place.

2Chronicles 7:14-15

Greatness begins with your ability to take control of your spiritual climate, and this can only happen if you are a prayerful person. The disciples, upon the realization of this crucial concept, came to Jesus and pleaded with him to teach them how to pray.

And it came to pass, that, as he was praying in a certain place, when he ceased, one of his disciples said unto him, Lord, teach us to pray, as John also taught his disciples.

Luke 11:1

I want to believe that when the disciples heard Him praying they realized that there is a way that He prays that makes him victorious over the powers of the enemy and life situations. They noticed that they did not have spiritual authority over the circumstances and situations in their lives the way He did. It is very important for us to realize that prayer is a spiritual weapon of God. When you pray you become offensive. When others are praying and you don't pray the demons of failure will come to your house. Mercy!

I remember during my university days, there were people who had written some prayers on papers and stuck them to the walls of their room. Every time before they slept they would point to one of the prayers on the wall and say "Father God this is my prayer for tonight" and they would curl up in bed and sleep without praying. This is playing it is not praying.

Satan uses some tactics to obstruct people from praying. One of those tactics is the spirit of slumber, which induces you to sleep when you are supposed to pray. The spirit of slumber brings heaviness that makes you sleep in your inner man. This happened to Peter, James and John. They slept while Jesus was praying.

Then cometh Jesus with them unto a place called Gethsemane, and saith unto the disciples, sit yee here, while I go and pray yonder. 37 And he took with him Peter and the two sons of Zebedee, and began to be sorrowful and very heavy. 38 Then saith he unto them, my soul is exceeding sorrowful, even unto death: tarry yee here, and watch with me. 39 And he went a little further, and fell on his face, and prayed, saying, O my Father, if it be possible, let this cup pass from me: nevertheless not as I will, but as thou *wilt*. 40 And he cometh unto the disciples, and findeth them asleep, and saith unto Peter, what, could ye not watch with me one hour? 41 Watch and pray, that ye enter not into temptation: the spirit indeed *is* willing, but the flesh *is* weak.

Mathew 26:36-41

Three men who slept when they were suppose to pray:

1. Peter denied Jesus three times because he didn't pray when he was supposed to pray.

People who don't pray deny their leaders and can even forsake their dreams and ambitions in life. When you slumber and fail in prayer you will be arrested later on in your life. You can't reach the desired destination of your life if you don't pray for it. I have come to realize that prayer is like depositing money in the bank, there will come a time that you need to withdraw from the prayers of yesterday, but if you didn't deposit prayer yesterday there will be nothing to withdraw today. Peter was arrested because he didn't pray when he was suppose to pray and the church had to come to his rescue and prayed for him.

And when he had apprehended him, he put *him* in prison, and delivered *him* to four quaternions of soldiers to keep him; intending after Easter to bring him forth to the people. 5 Peter therefore was kept in prison: but prayer was made without ceasing of the church unto God for him.

Acts 12:4-5

2. James was beheaded due to lack of prayer. When you don't pray the spirit of death

follows your life, in all areas of your life. The enemy wants to kill your vision, your dreams, your business, your calling, your marriage, your finances, your career and all that. I encourage you to rise up and invest in prayer and cover all areas of your life with prayer. The bible says we should pray without ceasing.

1 Now about that time Herod the king stretched forth *his* hands to vex certain of the church. 2 And he killed James the brother of John with the sword.

Acts 12:1-2

3. John didn't know there were spiritual forces which planned to remove his eyes, to cut off his vision and direction, he should have prayed but he slept instead. There are people who are in church with no eyes; they don't know where they are going, and what they want in life. Even when God has given them a powerful man of God they can't see or even receive direction from him. It is the spirit of slumber. You are walking around while you are yet sleeping in the inner man. May you

rise up and start taking prayer seriously.

The spirit of slumber comes from hell to disarm the children of God. It causes man to disconnect from God. It is very possible to walk around when you are sleeping in your spirit or in the inside.

Why does the enemy target your prayer life?

1) The altar of prayer is the platform for spiritual empowerment.
2) It is the secret of domain for the saint's empowerment.
3) It is a must for the devil to surrender if you are empowered in prayer. Because when you are empowered he will be under your feet.

Continuous lack of commitment to prayer will allow the spirit of slumber to come on you by God.

(According as it is written, God hath given them the spirit of slumber, eyes that they should not see, and ears that they should not hear ;) unto this day.

Romans 11:8

The instructions of the word of God against the spirit of slumber;

1. Awake from sleep and be given to light. When you are asleep in the inner man you are helpless.

   Wherefore he saith, Awake thou that sleepest, and arise from the dead, and Christ shall give thee light.

   Ephesians 5: 14

2. Give no sleep to your spiritual eyes. When you pray you deliver yourself from poverty, ancestral spirits, demonic spirits, spirits of divorce, spirits of failure etc.

   Give not sleep to thine eyes, nor slumber to thine eyelids. 5 Deliver thyself as a roe from the hand *of the hunter,* and as a bird from the hand of the fowler. 6 Go to the ant, thou sluggard; consider her ways, and be wise:

   Proverbs 6:4-5

3. Awake put on your faith, lose yourself from your capturer. You shall awake and stand by the pillar to destroy your enemy.

1 Awake, awake; put on thy strength, O Zion; put on thy beautiful garments, O Jerusalem, the holy city: for henceforth there shall no more come into thee the uncircumcised and the unclean. 2 Shake thyself from the dust; arise, *and* sit down, O Jerusalem: loose thyself from the bands of thy neck, O captive daughter of Zion.

Isaiah 52:1-2

Samson was captured while he was sleeping and his hair, which was the source of his power and strength, was taken.

13 And Delilah said unto Samson, hitherto thou hast mocked me, and told me lies: tell me where thou mightest be bound. And he said unto her, if thou weavest the seven locks of my head with the web... 19 And she made him sleep upon her knees; and she called for a man, and she caused him to shave off the seven locks of his head; and she began to afflict him, and his strength went from him.

Judges 16: 13 & 19

Delilah here represents the messengers of Satan. If you sleep and don't pray the enemy will take your source of strength and power and all that you intend to achieve in life will only remain as a wish.

Why is it dangerous to sleep on the altar of prayer?

❖ The enemy will plant his evil poisonous seeds of pain and failure in your life while you are sleeping.

But while men slept, his enemy came and sowed tares among the wheat, and went his way.

Matthew 13:25

❖ Enemies enter your closet and steal your things or possessions or joy or peace while you are sleeping. You can even lose your integrity as result.

Moreover, my father, see, yea, see the skirt of thy robe in my hand: for in that I cut off the skirt of thy robe, and killed thee not, know thou and see that *there is* neither evil nor transgression in

mine hand, and I have not sinned against thee; yet thou huntest my soul to take it.

1 Samuel 24:11

David entered King Saul's tent while he slept, and he could have just easily killed him. The spirit of slumber is very dangerous. Jesus said pray that you do not enter into temptations. On the journey to greatness prayer remains paramount. Resist the spirit of slumber which comes from the enemy to stop you from praying for your future. One man of God once said everyone who endeavours to go far in life, must pray continuously for hundred hours for their future and I believe in such type of things.

Who hath heard such a thing? Who hath seen such things? Shall the earth be made to bring forth in one day? *or* shall a nation be born at once? for as soon as Zion travailed, she brought forth her children.

Isaiah 66:8

Travail in prayer and you shall give birth to greatness in your life.

You could be asking yourself a million dollar

question; how do I pray effectively? The most powerful prayers you can ever pray involves the process of meditation. Let me take you through that process.

1. **Internalisation** – this is the time one takes studying the word of God and gathering scriptures in the area that they want to deal with in prayer. You cannot go to war without the necessary weapons that is suicidal. This is the time when you make the word of God your word; this is because God is only committed to his word.

For I am the Lord: I will speak, and the word that I shall speak shall come to pass; it shall be no more prolonged; for in your days, O rebellious house, will I say the word, and will perform it, saith the Lord God.

Ezekiel 12:25

This book of the law shall not depart out of thy mouth; but thou shalt meditate therein day and night, that thou mayest observe to do according to all that is written therein: for then thou shalt make thy way prosperous, and then thou shalt have good

success.

Joshua 1:8

Search the scriptures for the mind of God concerning your situation.

2. **Visualisation** – This is the stage in prayer that involves formation of mental pictures. It is very necessary that you allow the word of God to paint a picture in the canvass of your heart. These pictures are necessary to help you brace yourself in your faith and reach out for them. Engaging the mind through the power of imagination in prayer is a powerful thing to do.

Therefore I say unto you, what things soever ye desire, when ye pray, believe that ye receive them, and ye shall have them.

Mark 11:24

And the lord said, Behold, the people is one, and they have all one language; and this they begin to do: and now nothing will be restrained from them, which they have imagined to do.

Genesis 11:6

3. **Verbalisation** – This is part of prayer where

you begin speaking words to create in the natural what you are already seeing in the realm of your imagination. This is time to apply what we learned in chapter four about the power of the tongue.

13 We having the same spirit of faith, according as it is written, I believed, and therefore have I spoken; we also believe, and therefore speak; 14 Knowing that he that raised up the Lord Jesus shall raise up us also by Jesus, and shall present us with you.

2 Corinthians 4:13-14

This is the part of prayer that many people think it is prayer, but this part of prayer will not be effective if you don't engage the other processes. Don't just make noise be effective.

4. **Actualisation** – This is the stage of prayer where you move into a practical mode of receiving the things that you believe God for. The latter part of the following scripture says that when you pray believe that you receive and you have what you are praying for.

Therefore I say unto you, what things soever ye desire, when ye pray, believe that ye receive them, and ye shall have them.

Mark 11:24

I believe that as you pray the right way all your dreams and desires that you want accomplish shall come your way. The reason why it's critical to first consult the word of God is to help you not pray against God's word. The bible has this to say about people who do not pray according to God's word.

1 From whence come wars and fighting among you? 2 Ye lust, and have not: ye kill, and desire to have, and cannot obtain: ye fight and war, yet ye have not, because ye ask not. 3 Ye ask, and receive not, because ye ask amiss, that ye may consume it upon your lusts.

James 4:1-3

The last verse says it is possible to ask amiss so you don't just want to start making noise without checking first with the word of God whether your ambitions and dreams are lined up with the word of God so that you pray accurately and produce results in your life. I see the spirit of prayer coming upon you now in Jesus name.

May the Lord take you to greater heights as you pray and give you a testimony of greatness that will inspire someone to believe God for their own dreams in Jesus name.

Final Word

I believe the principles outlined in this manuscript have been helpful to you. My desire and prayer is that you should not just be a hearer but a doer also. Do something about what you have learned from this book and I believe the Lord will give you testimonies.

Finally I want to say that many hours have gone into this project and all this was done with you in mind. May God richly bless you and keep you on *the Journey to greatness.*
Shalom

Prayer of Salvation

That if thou shall confess with thy mouth the Lord Jesus, and shalt believe in thine heart that God hath raised him from the dead, thou shalt be saved.

Romans 10:9

If you don't know Jesus as your personal Lord and saviour you can pray the following prayer from the bottom of your heart and Jesus will save your soul.

Dear God in heaven, I come to you in the name of Jesus. I acknowledge to You that I am a sinner, and I am sorry for my sins and the life that I have lived; I need your forgiveness.

I believe that your only begotten Son Jesus Christ shed His precious blood on the cross at Calvary and died for my sins, and I am now willing to turn from my sins.

You said in Your Holy Word, Romans 10:9 that if we confess the Lord our God and believe in our hearts that God raised Jesus from the dead, we shall be saved.

Right now I confess Jesus as the Lord of my soul. With my heart, I believe that God raised Jesus from the dead. This very moment I accept Jesus Christ as my own personal Saviour and according to His Word, right now I am saved.

Thank you, Jesus, for your unlimited grace which has saved me from my sins. Therefore, Lord Jesus, transform my life so that I may bring glory and honour to you alone and not to myself.

Thank you Jesus, for dying for me, and giving me eternal life. Amen.

You are now a child of God, look for a church that preaches the truth of God's word and join it so that you can grow in your faith. If you want to contact us you can email or call us on the numbers provided for at beginning of this book.

Stay blessed.

FAITH COVENANT MINISTRIES
INTERNATIONAL
P.O.Box 46115 Gaborone. Botswana | (+267) 74 959 306 | (+267) 71 532 284

Reaching the lost and Maturing the Saints